"The Weatherman Is Coming To My School Today"

Written by
CHRISTOPHER NANCE

Illustrated by
ARDAVAN & KHASHAYAR JAVID

First Edition

Text copyright © 1997 by Christopher Nance
Christopher Productions, Inc.
CPI Publishers © copyright 1997

Printed in the United States of America
IPF Printing, Burbank, CA

Published by
Christopher Productions, Inc.
CPI Publishers
10153½ Riverside Drive #266
Toluca Lake, CA 91602
(818) 831-9268

ISBN 0-9648363-7-8
LIBRARY OF CONGRESS CATALOG CARD NUMBER — 97-91584

Acknowledgments

Special thanks to Dr. Louella Benson-Garcia for helping in the Editing of this book.

Special thanks to Paul Villar, my Personal Assistant and Publisher, for all the hard work and long hours.

Special thanks to my darling Sam. My Editor, Publisher and best friend.

To all the boys and girls at the hundreds of schools, who invited me to present my "LET'S TALK WEATHER," program at their schools. You are the future, so always do your best.

One day, not too long ago, Shannon was sitting
in front of the television set, eating her breakfast
and eagerly watching the morning news.
Her eyes suddenly got big! She jumped up,
let out a scream and ran through the house.

Little Shannon was very excited as she rushed into her parents' bedroom.

"What is it, Dear?" her mother asked with a look of worry in her eyes.

Shannon was so excited she could hardly catch her breath.

"Mom the Weatherman mentioned my name on TV, he said he's coming to my school today."

Her mother was certain that it could not be.

"Oh, I think the Weatherman is too busy to visit your school, Sweetheart, but you are going to be late for school unless you hurry."

"But Mom!"

Shannon was so surprised by her mother's reply, she couldn't move.

". . . and don't forget your sweater," her mother insisted.

Little Shannon did as she was told, but as she turned off the television set and carried her breakfast dishes to the sink, she had to wonder if her ears were playing tricks.

"I did hear the Weatherman say he was coming to my school today," she said out loud as she pulled on her sweater and reached for the front doorknob.

Shannon called out to her mother, "Goodbye Mom, I love you."
The door slammed shut behind her.

On her way to school, Shannon could not get her legs to move fast enough. She was certain that the Weatherman said he was coming to her school today. After all, she had written him five letters inviting him to her school.

The playground was filled with children. The first bell had not rung, so Shannon ran to the parking lot and waited.

"Hi Shannon, what are you looking for and why are you waiting here? asked her friend Bobby, a boy from class.

"I'm waiting to see what kind of car the Weatherman is driving," she replied.

RRRRRIIIIIIINNNNNNNGGGGGGGGGG!

As Shannon was waiting, the first bell rang and students started running for their classrooms.

"Bye Shannon, see you in class." Without waiting for Shannon's reply, Bobby dashed off across the playground, heading toward the classroom.

Shannon let out a sigh, turned away from the parking lot and slowly walked toward the same classroom.

"Better move faster than that . . ." said Mr. Reed, the friendly custodian, "or you'll be late for class."

Shannon liked Mr. Reed. He was a jolly man and always had a kind word for Shannon. As she stepped up her pace, she called out to the custodian.

"Did you hear the Weatherman on television say he was coming to our school today?"

Mr. Reed thought for a moment. He then answered, **"I can't say that I did Shannon, my TV set is broken."**

Shannon let out another sigh. She reached her classroom just as the final bell rang.

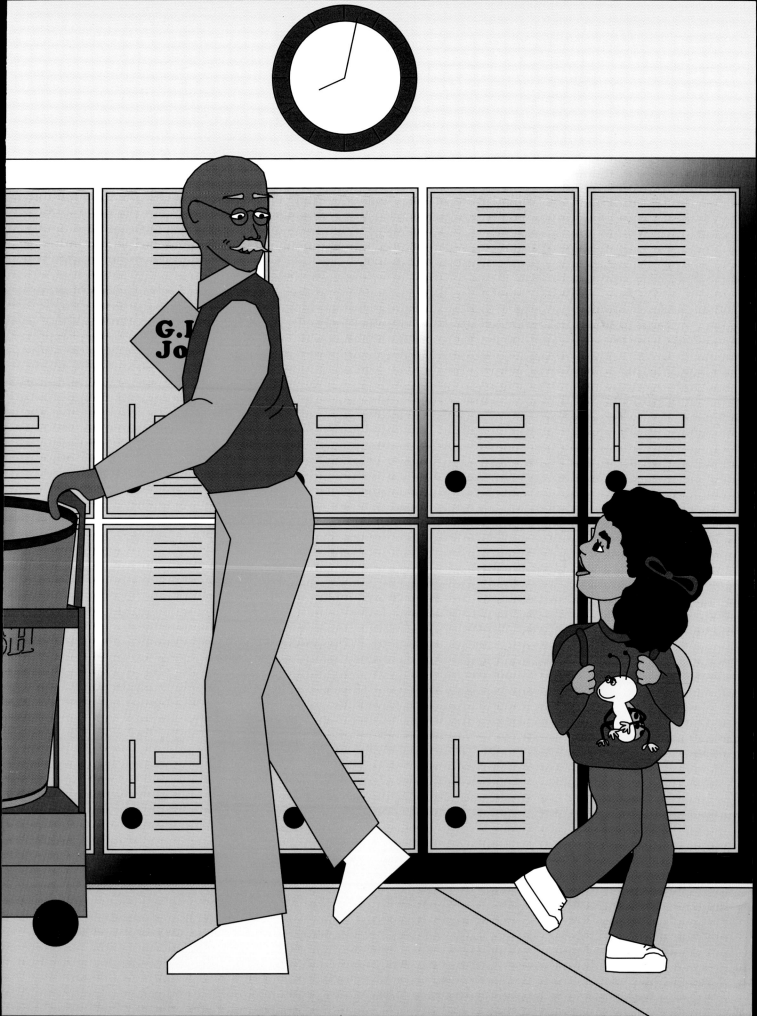

Shannon's teacher was Mr. Karr. If anyone knew if the Weatherman was coming to her school today, he would. So before Mr. Karr had a chance to clear his throat and quiet the children down, Shannon's hand flew into the air and the words just seemed to blast out of her mouth like a rocket.

"Mr. Karr, what time is the Weatherman coming to our school today?"

The class fell silent. Heads started to turn toward Shannon and she could feel her face turning red.

"This was not a good idea," she said under her breath, but before she could pull her hand down, the damage was already done and she could not bring back the words.

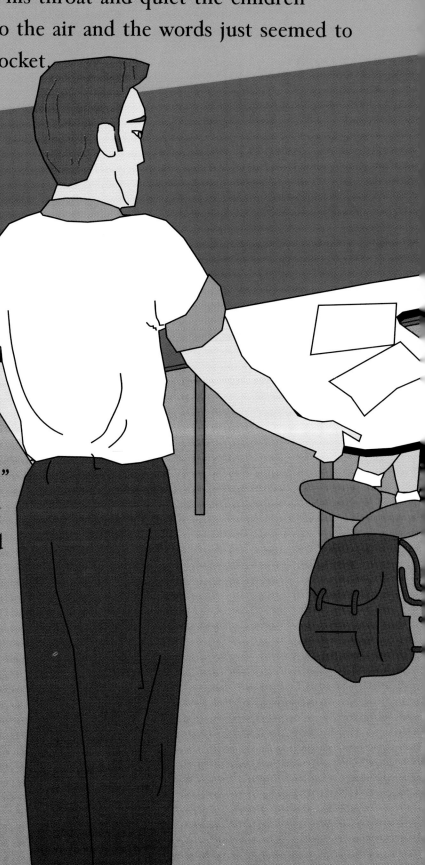

"**What did you say Shannon?**" asked Mr. Karr. Shannon was too embarrassed to repeat her question, but as the class waited, she knew she had to say something.

"**Is the Weatherman coming to our school today?**" Now all the students' attention turned to Mr. Karr and they eagerly waited for an answer.

"**Shannon, why would the Weatherman come to our small school?**"

That's when all the children started to laugh. They were laughing at Shannon. She felt terrible. Even her friend Bobby couldn't hold back his giggles. Mr. Karr could see how Shannon felt, so he loudly clapped his hands together to restore some order. But not before one of the boys yelled out, "**The next thing she'll tell us is the President is going to drop by for cookies and milk.**"

This time the class laughed harder and louder. Shannon wanted to hide from everyone.

"That's enough!" boomed Mr. Karr.

"We'll have no more talk about the Weatherman, or the President visiting our school today." The class became silent.

TRASH

Mr. Karr led the class through a reading exercise. Time passed quickly, but not quick enough for Shannon. During recess, a few of her classmates continued to tease her. The day was going from bad to worse.

"Shannon, walk with me for a while," said Mr. Karr. Shannon froze. She knew she was in trouble and her heart started pounding like a drum.

"I'm sorry, Mr. Karr."

But before Shannon could say any more, Mr. Karr stopped her.

"I can tell you have something on your mind. Do you want to talk about it?"

Shannon wanted to cry, but she took a big breath and started at the beginning.

"I wrote the Weatherman 5 letters weeks ago and invited him to come to our school. I drew a map and showed him how to get here."

A tear fell from Shannon's eye.

"Did you hear from him?" Mr. Karr asked.

"I received a thank-you note and an autographed picture that I have on my wall, but he did not say when he would come. This morning on television, I heard him say my name and that he was coming to our school today."

Mr. Karr put his arm around Shannon and told her that he would call the TV station and talk to the Weatherman at the end of the school day.

"I do have some advice for you." Shannon looked up at her teacher. "Believe in yourself. Your ears are as good as anyone's, and so are your eyes. If you heard the Weatherman say he was coming to our school, then that is what you heard. Do not let someone make you doubt your senses or yourself. You are a perfect person. Do not let people's jokes, teasing or laughter cause you to doubt yourself."

The bell rang and recess was over. Shannon felt better after her talk with Mr. Karr. The two walked back to the classroom side by side. Her classmates ran past them and found their seats.

Little Shannon tried to keep her mind on her studies, but she kept thinking about the Weatherman. She was certain he had announced on the television this morning that he was coming to her school today.

Just then, the classroom door opened and in walked the Principal, Ms. Vara.

"Please forgive the interruption Mr. Karr, but may I speak to Shannon for a moment?"

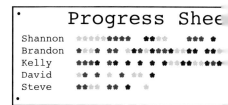

Progress Shee				
Shannon	★★★★★★★★	★★		★★★ ★
Brandon	★★★ ★★	★★★ ★★★★★★	★★ ★★	
Kelly	★★★★ ★★	★ ★ ★ ★ ★★★★	★★★	★★★
David	★★ ★ ★ ★	★		
Steve	★★★ ★★ ★	★		

Fear rushed over Shannon. She felt she was in trouble again, and so did the rest of the class. All eyes were on Shannon as she slowly stood up and walked past her classmates. Her heart was pounding again and she felt as though she was on fire.

Shannon slowly followed the principal out of the classroom and down the hall. She was looking down, when she bumped into the leg of a tall man.

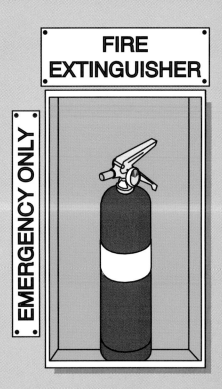

"You must be Shannon." The voice was familiar to her, and when she looked up, she could hardly believe her eyes.

It was the Weatherman and he was right in front of her, wearing a big smile.

"I knew it!" Shannon cried with joy. "I knew I heard you say you were coming. I told them, but everyone laughed at me."

The Weatherman got down on one knee and was face to face with Shannon as he took her hand.

"Let's go back inside your class and see who's laughing now."

A big smile brightened Shannon's face.

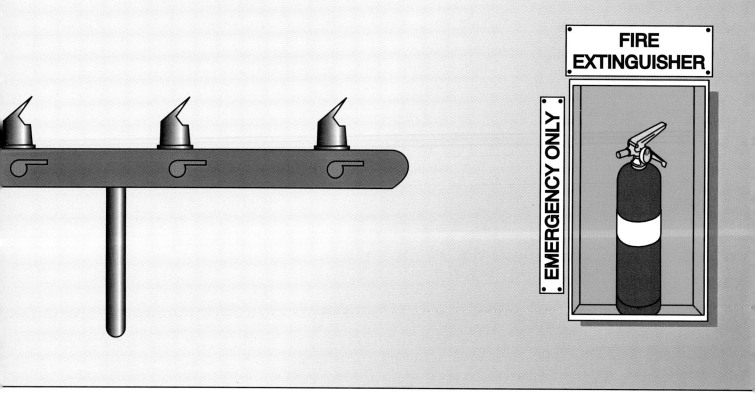

"Gee, I wish my mother was here, she didn't believe me either," Shannon said.

Ms. Vara laughed, "You two go inside, I'll call your Mom and tell her to come to school. We have a surprise for her."

Shannon took the Weatherman's hand and walked with him down the hall past the other classrooms. All the other children watched and their mouths dropped wide open.

THE END

HOW MANY OF MY BOOKS HAVE YOU ALREADY READ?

❑ *MUHAMMAD AND THE MARATHON*

❑ *BEFORE THERE WERE PEOPLE*

❑ *THE WEATHERMAN IS COMING TO MY SCHOOL TODAY*

BOOK ORDERS

To inquire about purchasing
this book or other books by
Christopher Nance
Call or write to (818) 831-9268

Christopher Productions, Inc.
10153½ Riverside Drive #266
Toluca Lake, California 91602

We accept VISA, Master Card, or American Express.
Please do not send cash.
Make checks payable to: CPI
Returned checks are subject to a service charge for the greater of $15
or maximum allowed by state law.

BOOK SIGNINGS

Please contact us at the above phone number or address if you are having
a large book fair at your school, church, or organization and would like
Christopher Nance to attend for a book signing.

FAN CLUB & NEWSLETTER

If you'd like to join Christopher Nance's fan club, **"The Weather Dudes"**,
and be included in our mailing list to receive a newsletter, send the following
information to our office:

Name (First and Last):
Address:
Age:
Birthday: